A PLOT OF MURDER

A Murder Mystery Comedy Play

Lee Mueller

Play Dead Murder Mystery Plays

CONTENTS

Title Page
Copyright
Preface
Characters
ACT I 1
ACT 2 31
Afterword 49
Books By This Author 51

Copyright © 2008 Lee Mueller

All rights reserved

The characters and events portrayed in this book are fictitious. Any similarity to real persons, living or dead, is coincidental and not intended by the author.

No part of this book may be reproduced, or stored in a retrieval system, or transmitted in any form or by any means, electronic, mechanical, photocopying, recording, or otherwise, without express written permission of the publisher.

ISBN-13: 978-1493702787
ISBN-10: 1493702785

Cover design by: L' Anians
Library of Congress Control Number: 2018675309
Printed in the United States of America

PREFACE

Caution: Professionals and amateurs are hereby advised that A PLOT OF MURDER is subject to a royalty. It is fully protected under the copyright laws of the United States of America and of all countries covered by International Copyright union (including the Dominion of Canada and the rest of the British Commonwealth) and of all countries covered by the Pan-American Copyright Convention and the Universal Copyright, and of all countries with which the United States has reciprocal copyright relations. All rights including professional, amateur, motion picture, recitation, lecturing, public reading, radio broadcasting, television, video or sound taping, all other forms of mechanical or electronic reproduction, such as information storage and retrieval systems and photocopying, and the rights of translation into foreign languages, are strictly reserved. All inquiries concerning rights should be addressed to Playedwell, LLC - play-dead.com.

CHARACTERS

George Holmes- has selective hearing issues he blames on his hearing aid. Older man and is president of the Neighborhood Board.

Fannie Mae- George's younger attractive wife. Works as a real estate agent and pretty much wears the pants in the family.

Lars Cuttovich- Board member of HOA. Young man running his own landscaping business.

Ella Adler- Board member of HOA. Older resident but young at heart.

Lou Braunhorst- Upright citizen of the neighborhood and follower of most conspiracy theories. Tries to maintain an intellectual demeanor to cover his paranoia -but often fails with malapropisms

Ethyl Cornwirtz- Senior citizen on a fixed income.

Charlie Ratcliff- Councilman for the area, quick with doublespeak and spinning issues as well as part-time Elvis impersonator.

Eric Lawson- New resident of the neighborhood and new Law Student with fresh ideas.

Trish Lawson- Eric's outspoken and protective wife.

Agent McManshon - Secret Federal Agent that enjoys keeping things a secret.

Tanya- Councilman Ratcliff's young assistant.

ACT I

The setting is a meeting of the Fleur Estates Manor Association (FEMA). The four board members are at the front preparing themselves for the start of the meeting.

The residents are mingling and complaining to each other about various issues large and small, ie. property tax increases, Utility prices and about other residents of the neighborhood.

The board: George, Fannie Mae, Lars, Ella will be seated at a long table -(on the stage or if not performed on a stage - at head/front of room.) If possible -have one working microphone for several characters to use.

The other cast Ethyl, Lou, Eric and Trish will be seated at various points in the audience.

Ratcliff and Tanya should be seating in the back.

GEORGE stands up from the table and with a microphone. He begins speaking but is very much inaudible since he has not turned the Microphone "on".

FANNIE MAE comes from the back - halfway up and

stops -

FANNIE MAE: GEORGE! GEORGE! (*she mimes the microphone with her hand and points to it*) Turn on the button! The button! Turn it on! We can't hear you.

GEORGE: What? I can't hear you.

FANNIE MAE: Exactly! Turn the *switch* on! The *mic*!

GEORGE: You switched with Mike?

LARS stands up from the table, reaches over and turns on Microphone.

LARS: (*into Microphone*) Test test. There you go, Mr. Holmes! (*sits back down*)

GEORGE: Oh. (*He holds the microphone very close when he speaks causing loud distorted sound*) TEST.. Test.. One..Two....I WOULD LIKE TO CALL TO ORDER THE NEIGHBORHOOD ASSOCIATION OF THE FLEUR ESTATES...

FANNIE MAE: GEORGE! You're too CLOSE! Back away from the Microphone!

GEORGE: The phone? Take a message, I've got to get this meeting started.

LARS stands back up and physically moves GEORGE's arm so the microphone is away from his mouth. George is not quite sure what is going on.

LARS: There you go, Mr. Holmes!

ACT I 3

GEORGE: Uh.. check. I would like to.. can you hear me? (*wait for response*) I would like to call to the ... (*picks up clipboard and has trouble balancing microphone and the clipboard at the same time -tries to hold both in same hand etc.*)..to call the... the... to order the Fleur Estates HOA meeting. Roll call of board members, Fannie Mae Hathaway Holmes?

FANNIE MAE: Present.

GEORGE: Lars Cuttovich?

LARS: I'm here.

GEORGE: Ella Adler.

ELLA: Yes.

GEORGE: May the record reflect all in attendance. Secretary Lars has submitted the minutes from the last meeting which will be submitted into the record. All those in favor?

BOARD MEMBERS Aye.

GEORGE: All those opposed? Second item is the matter of the trash pick up service. Our contract will expire at midnight next fiscal quarter. Suggestions for retaining our present service or accepting contracts for a new service..

LOU: (*stands and interrupts*) Let's cut the *trash* talk and move on to the real issue! And that's the issue of local council pushing this "element remains" on the common grounds on our lots!

GEORGE: *Lots* of what?

LOU: Lots of trouble Georgie boy! I happen to have certain information about this deal. I know a guy who has a friend, whose cousin works for the council. Serves coffee or something. Anyway, if this deal goes through, they're gunna restablish a Strip Mall and Family Fun Pizza Palace next to our homes! I don't know about you, but the last thing I want is a buncha loud screaming yahoos in the area!

GEORGE: What's streaming on yahoo?

FANNIE MAE: Never mind George, it's just Lou, please continue.

GEORGE: Oh sure. Right. Let's see. (*checks clipboard*)

ELLA: (*stands*) Lou has a point! I for one, feel the Association has a right to know about this!

FANNIE MAE: In due time Ella! George! Please continue!

GEORGE: Let's see.. did I do the trash service? Or the matter of the Construction sign in Francis Farmer's yard? Apparently, there is a rule about signs obstructing curb appeal.

LOU: I gotta sign for you! And it's a bad sign!

GEORGE: There can be no signs, bad or otherwise placed in anyone's yard. Next issue..

LOU: Is the issue of the board sitting around letting this

ACT I

happen!

GEORGE: ..the grass in the (Maguilicutty)[1] lawn is beyond the required 2 3/4 inch length..

ETHYL: I think it's disgraceful!

LARS: (*stands*) You're right Ethyl it is! As most of you know I have a lawn care business. If the Maguilicuttys' had contracted me to take care of their grass, it would always measure up to..

FANNIE MAE: Lars! Please! What have I told you about soliciting during Board time. George, if you would.

(*LARS sits*)

GEORGE: ..and the issue of the Bass Boat in Bubba Morganthaler's driveway. As you know there is an issue in the bylaws...

ETHYL: Whoever heard of such a thing? I mean, what is this world coming to?

LARS: What Ethyl? The bylaws about boats?

ETHYL: Why no! I mean, having a Family Fun Pizza Palace in the neighborhood! What kind of undesirables would that attract?

LARS: I don't know... Families? Children?

ETHYL: And what about that Strip Club? It's one thing to have screaming kids, but to have strippers parading around...

FANNIE MAE: A strip *mall*, Ethyl. Not a Strip club! Completely different type of business!

GEORGE: And so, for any new business..

LOU: There we go! *New business!* Now, let's address this remnant remain thing.

FANNIE MAE: *Eminent domain*, Lou! It's called eminent domain!

LOU: Yea? You say potato and I say tomato. As I said, I know a guy who knows a guy..

FANNIE MAE: Would this be the same guy who told you about the Secret Black Helicopters hovering over your house?

LOU: No! (*beat*) Maybe. Hey don't laugh! I seen them Black Helicopters up there! Late at night - buzzin' my Oak trees out back. They're shooting indivisible laser beams at my satellite dish that carry signals that skew my Fair and Balanced news programs! Puts a liberal spin on everything! But that's another story! The point is this! (*walks toward RATCLIFF*) Our very own neighbor, Consolerman Ratcliffe is behind this whole Enemal Dominance thing! Ain't that right?

Ratcliff seated and dressed like Elvis, tries to be inconspicuous.

RATCLIFF: I really don't have the time, I have another function very soon..

LOU: Hey! What's with the get-up?

RATCLIFF: Well, I uh... you'll have to excuse my appearance..

TANYA: He's part of All The King's Men singing group at Elvis O Rama tonight.

LOU: Sure he is. (*to surrounding audience*) If 'the King' here does it 'his way', then four-eighths of our sub-dervison will be gone by in six months' time. Now that should get you "all shook up"!

GEORGE: (*to LARS*) So, is there any 'new' business?

LARS: New business? Yea, I just gave the Michaels a bid on trimming the shrubs. Oh Lou!, that reminds me! Mrs. Michaels asked me to give you the acorns that fell from *your* trees into *her* yard. They're out in my truck. Remind me and I'll give 'em to you before you go.

LOU: Acorns? Now, wait a minute! I know my rights and "possession" is ten-ninths of the law! So, if old lady Michaels was in possession of those acorns then by law, they belong to her! That's how it works!

ELLA: Speaking of laws, isn't there a law about creating a ruckus during certain hours of the morning?! Lars is forever out at the crack of dawn running that blasted leaf whacker!

LARS: Sorry Ella, but it's my busy time of the year.

FANNIE MAE: Ella! Lars! Take this up during the break!

We need to get on with some of the more pressing issues! *(beat)* George? Get us back on track, please.

ETHYL: And another thing, what's with that old railroad track that runs along Maple (*or insert local name*) Street? I hear they're converting it into a bike path! I don't want kids riding bikes behind my house. What will that do to the property values? I'm on a fixed income! We never had bike paths when I was young. They should ride in the street where they belong!

During this Fannie Mae goes up and takes Microphone from GEORGE

FANNIE MAE: Ethyl, please. It's not the time for questions and concerns from the floor. It *could* be time, but someone let this meeting get out of hand. *(looks at George)* You'll have to wait, we have a lot of business to cover...

LOU: So what about covering this Element Romaine business?

FANNIE MAE: Lou, I just said, we only a certain amount of time..

LOU: I think it's *time* to cover this business.

FANNIE MAE: In due time Lou.

LOU: I think it's time we do!

FANNIE MAE: Do what Lou?

LOU: Do time. I mean, it's time we do.. the business

that's due... and we do it now. Now is the time we do it. It's due now.

FANNIE MAE: What are you talking about Lou?

LOU: I'm talking about what I *been* talking about! This Evident Dominion that Ratcliffe and his cronies are pushing through law!

FANNIE MAE: Lou, I'm going to have to rule that subject out of order. It's not on the agenda this evening, ergo, it's *out of order.*

LOU: Now wait, now what?

FANNIE MAE: Let me to this letter from legal counsel. (*she pulls from pocket and reads*) "Any reference to proposed real estate transactions would be speculative, ergo deemed heresy under the bylaws of the Trustee agenda. Since speculation - at this point is a non-actuality, it shall not be submitted or discussed as business. Therefore must be deemed as out of order."

ELLA: Now hold on a minute! Point of order here Fannie Mae! Who are *you* to rule something 'out of order'! Only the President of the board can rule something out of order!

FANNIE MAE: I'm the president's wife. (*snaps her fingers*) George!

GEORGE: Huh?

FANNIE MAE: The letter from legal counsel, remember? The matter we discussed? The heresy matter?

GEORGE: What does who say matter?

FANNIE MAE: Do you have your hearing aid turned off again? The LETTER George! Remember?! (*dangles letter in front of his face*)

GEORGE: Right! Oh yes, yes, that. Right. (*clears throat*) Regarding the matter per the letter, I will have to uh... have to uh...

FANNIE MAE: Rule it out of order.

GEORGE: Right, right. I will have to.. hereby, rule this out of order.

FANNIE MAE: So let's move on to other business. George, if you would like to continue.

LOU: So what just happened?

ELLA: That's what I would like to know! Why is this the first time we are hearing about this letter?

FANNIE MAE: Well, perhaps it's because - this is the first time it has come up.

LOU: No it ain't. I brought it up a few minutes ago. This'd be the *second* time it came up.

FANNIE MAE: No matter when it came up, it's out of order and out of our hands. We need to move on.

LOU: We'll all be 'moving on' if this happens. They'll be bulldozing down our domesticals!

ETHYL: Bulldozing?

LOU: That's right Ethyl! Say sayonara to your garden. Toodeloo to your bell peppers and 'mater plants. Ah-ree-va-dee-ohs to your lilies and your cro-santa- minimums. All gone! We won't have to fret over Magillicutty's lawn or Bubba's bass boat. Or even that the McDaniels leave their Christmas Lights up well into July! Who cares? It'll all be ash-fault and see-meant.

LARS: On the bright side Lou, that will take care of your acorn problem.

LOU: Yea? And it'll take care of your land-scraper business too!

LARS: Oh yea. Oh wow. Not cool.

FANNIE MAE: If you want to discuss this subject, you need to do so, outside the confines of this meeting.

LOU: Yes! I want to discuss this! (*starts walking to exit*) Tell me where these 'confines' are, so I can go there!

FANNIE MAE: No, Lou! "Outside the confines" of this meeting.

LOU: Right! I'm going outside.

LARS: Hey Lou! If you're going outside, let me get your acorns! (*Lars runs out and exits*)

FANNIE MAE: Not the literal 'outside' Lou. Not outside *outside*! Just outside of *this meeting*.

LOU: Well, if this meeting is '*inside*', how can I be outside of it if I'm inside. The only way to be 'outside' is to be outside *outside!* Not here inside *inside.*

ELLA: This is just foolishness! This inside outside business is neither here nor there.

FANNIE MAE: Lou Braunhorst! This is a dead issue. I must insist you come to order and take your seat!

LOU: *You* take a seat!

ERIC LAWSON stands.

ERIC: Excuse me, if I may address the board, I'm Eric Lawson at 419. I just wanted to submit something here...

FANNIE MAE: The board recognizes the man from 419.

LOU: (*looking at Eric*) Well, I don't.

FANNIE MAE: Go ahead, Mr. Lawson.

ERIC: Thank you. While I realize this board has certain procedures you must abide by, I believe there is an amendment in the HOA bylaws, called the "Circumstantial Emergency Amendment." I may be paraphrasing but I believe it states that any 'introduced business' which affects the overall *well being* of the community, shall take precedence and *not* be subject to rulings of the governing board. Including outside counsel.

LOU: I couldn't have said it better myself.

ELLA: You couldn't have said it at all.

FANNIE MAE: O.K. And what's your point, Mr. Lawson?

LOU: It's as plain as the nose on your face! He's saying that the business of the.. overall being is .. introduced and the... circumcision amendment are... what was it?

ELLA: Told you.

ERIC: The point is, the business of *Eminent Domain*, does in fact, affect the well being of the community. Therefore, any rulings by the board, specifically your "out of order" ruling, does not apply.

FANNIE MAE: Mr. Lawson, as I stated. I have a letter from legal counsel that states...

ERIC: Yes, I know. But *your* own amendment negates the letter from legal counsel. You can't use it. I think everyone in this room would agree that the potential of our homes being "taken away or bulldozed", for lack of better terms is in fact - a "Circumstantial Emergency" and much be treated as such.

FANNIE MAE: (*sighs*) I see.

ERIC: I'm merely stating your *own* rules.

LOU: Ha! Lookie there! Your own rules outdid your overrules! Is this a great country or what?

ELLA: So the *out of order*, is no longer out of order?

LOU: Yea. I don't need to go outside to the confines! I can stay right here.

FANNIE MAE: George? (*beat*) George! We need a ruling on this.

GEORGE: I'm not drooling. (*wiping his mouth in case*)

FANNIE MAE: Oh for the love of Pete!

GEORGE: You're in love with Pete?! I thought it...

FANNIE MAE: Councilman Ratcliff? Could I... could we have a little help with this?

RATCLIFF stands up.

RATCLIFF: Yes, well.. again, if you'll excuse my appearance. I'm not normally dressed in such a way. As my assistant stated earlier, there is a function... "Elvis-o-rama" going on tonight and..

LOU: Big Deal-O-Rama! Your function now is telling us why you sold us out!

RATCLIFF: Well, you see, I would need a clear definition of the term 'sold'. So, it's not as simple as at that.

ELLA: Well what's it "as simple as"?

LOU: You need to start simply fessin up Ratcliff! Explain to the people what your intentions are!

RATCLIFF: I would be happy to explain everything, however, I would need clarification on the use of the word "intentions." And as I was saying, unfortunately, if I don't leave shortly...

(*starts crossing to exit - TANYA gets up and follows him*)

LOU: Ain't that somethin'? We can certainly see where your majorities lie!

RATCLIFF: I assure you, sir, I have the best interest of the association in mind. What is currently in the works will benefit all parties concerned. Within the realm of the matters presently at hand.. to put it simply. At this time, I need to be going. Thank you for the opportunity to address this matter, and I hope I've made my position clear. Thank you for your support and... good evening.

LOU: If that don't beat all! (*crosses and exits out of room/ theater*)

FANNIE MAE: Charlie, I mean, Councilmen Ratcliff is a very busy man and I am sure he would be happy to elaborate at some other time. Isn't that correct Councilmen?

RATCLIFF: Yes Fannie Mae, of course! Some other time. Yes indeed. Tell you what, my dear assistant Tanya.. will remain here tonight.. (*He takes her by shoulders and pushes her back toward into room*)

TANYA: Charlie!

RATCLIFF: ..and if you have any questions or concerns, she would be more than happy to note them and...relay them.. to me.. OK Tanya?

TANYA: You're kidding right?

RATCLIFF: (*quietly pleading*) Just hear their concerns and

uh.. you know.

TANYA: You've got a spot on your jumper.

RATCLIFF: What? (*looks down*) Well, bless my soul! What's wrong with me? (*starts to rub it with his fingers*)

TANYA: No! You'll make it worse! Gets some cold water. Dab it with some paper towels. Dab not rub.

RATCLIFF: Very well. (*louder to everyone*) So let Tanya know your issues and then first thing tomorrow...

TANYA: You have the groundbreaking tomorrow.

RATCLIFF: ..and then first thing Monday..

TANYA: Lions Club.

RATCLIFF: ..first thing Tuesday, I will...

TANYA: School board..

RATCLIFF: Eventually, I'll look over the issues and address them, OK? Good. (*to Tanya*) Where's the bathroom?

TANYA: Over there. (*or modify to your location*)

RATCLIFF: Thanks. (*quickly crossing -using this speech to cover*) So, yea, just go ahead and uh... do that, so then I can... you know... and very soon, we will... convene and explore the possibilities and the.. probabilities and have... uh... you know.. a thing. Thanks for your concern and.. (*in Elvis-ease*) Thank you very much! (*exits out back*)

TANYA will follow slowly behind and out of sight

ETHYL: Who's he supposed to be? Wayne Newton?

LARS: I think he's Elvis Costello.

ELLA: So does anybody care to explain what in the world is going on?

FANNIE MAE: Sure Ella, it's very simple, Councilman Ratcliff will address the issues at a later date. Since he is the one that knows the details, he's the only one that can shed some light.

ELLA: So till then, we're in the dark?

ETHYL: Will he address the bike path? That's what I wanna know about! You see, I'm on a fixed income. I don't get around like I used to and..

FANNIE MAE: He's not in charge of the bike path Ethyl, you'll have to contact the Parks department.

ETHYL: Oh fiddle! I have to use the little girls' room. (*exits*)

ELLA: Hold your horses Ethyl, I coming with you. Too much coffee and too much monkey business. (*exits*)

GEORGE: I'd like some more coffee.

FANNIE MAE: And I'd like to you to get the meeting resumed. Do you remember where you left off? "New business", I think.

GEORGE: You want to start a new business? I thought

you were happy in real estate.

FANNIE MAE: OK George, you're going to have to turn up your hearing aid! It's not cute anymore. It's starting to become annoying.

 FANNIE MAE reaches behind GEORGE'S ear and adjusts the device.

GEORGE: Holy mackerel woman! Watch what you're doing!!

FANNIE MAE: (*leaning down close to his ear*)Test! Test! Is this thing on?

GEORGE: Yes! Yes! It's on!

FANNIE MAE: Leave it on! And now get on with the meeting.

 George arranges his papers and lifts the microphone.

GEORGE: If the board will come to... (*looks around*) Where's the board? How can I continue if the board's not here?

FANNIE MAE: Gee George I don't know. Life and people move on when you're not listening when you don't have a clue.

GEORGE: Is that right? Well, I have a few clues.

FANNIE MAE: Oh do you really?

GEORGE: Yes I do. I'm fully aware of what's going on.

FANNIE MAE: Are you? Might I remind you, your term for as president only has 6 more months before the board must either re-elect you or appoint someone else.

GEORGE: And you my dear would *be* that someone else?

FANNIE MAE: Are you kidding me? They couldn't pay me enough to do your job.

ERIC: (*stands up*) Excuse me? Mrs. Holmes.

FANNIE MAE: Please, call me Fannie Mae.

ERIC: Sure. I was wondering if you had an idea when Councilman Ratcliff would address these issues?

FANNIE MAE: Lawson! Now I remember! The brick ranch with the two-car, architectural shingles and quarter-acre side lot!

ERIC: Yes. That's me, brick ranch two car.

FANNIE MAE: I was the listing agent on that property. If I recall you met three counteroffers. I like a man who knows what he wants and won't stop until he gets it.

TRISH Stands up hugs her Eric's arm tightly.

TRISH: I do as well. I'm MRS Lawson. Eric's wife. I designed the counteroffers.

FANNIE MAE: Oh. Did you now?

ERIC: Anyway, Trish and I were curious, how long the board was *aware* of this situation?

FANNIE MAE: Which situation is that?

TRISH: The situation where our properties were deemed not *economically viable*. I'm sure you know how eminent domain works, Mrs. Holmes!

FANNIE MAE: Not as such. Not totally.

TRISH: It's a fascinating game! A corporate giant needs real estate so, they look around, find something.. Oh look! There's already houses on it! But wait! We're a corporate giant! So? No problem! Make a few calls, pull a few strings, line a few pockets, and suddenly! Shazam! An entire community is declared "blighted".

FANNIE MAE: Really? Is that how it works? Fancy that!

TRISH: It is fancy. And dirty. And legal in some areas. But I'm sure you know Mrs. Holmes, you're in Real estate.

FANNIE MAE: Not totally, no. I mean, I'm familiar with some..

TRISH: Right! You're just a lowly agent. You should look into Real estate *development*. It' much more lucrative than silly old counter offers on 2 car ranches with architectural shingles, isn't it?

FANNIE MAE: Uh..yes..I'm sure it could be.

TRISH: Where else can you buy up land, cut down all the trees and then name the streets after them.

ERIC: You'll have to forgive my wife, she has certain

convictions and.. anyway, about this letter you had regarding the eminent domain matter, how long have you known about this?

FANNIE MAE: George? You want to field this one. I need to speak to uh... I need some air. (*she gets up and quickly exits*)

GEORGE: Uh.. (*reaching up behind his ear*) I'm sorry, the battery in this confounded thing is... what was the question?

TRISH: I think the real question is, who on the board has something to gain by this deal?

GEORGE: No. I don't think it will rain...

TRISH: I guess we don't need a weatherman to know which way the wind blows.

GEORGE: I think the board is taking a recess here. I'd be happy to hear about the 'choir' when we resume. If you'll excuse me. I have to see if I have a good battery for this thing... I'll be right back. (*crosses to exit out front*)

ERIC:(*looks around*) Where's Ratcliff's assistant Tanya?

TRISH: There she is. (*points to back*)

Trish and Eric cross to back with Tanya and silently engage in stage talk.

Just before George exits he bumps into SPECIAL INVESTIGATOR MCMANSHON who is coming in.

GEORGE: I'm sorry. Excuse me.

MCMANSHON: Quite alright. No harm done.

McManshon looks around -as if looking for a particular person. Approaches a random table. LARS re-enters.

MCMANSHON: Excuse me, is this the H.O.A meeting? (*ad-lib based on response and then*) Do you know if Councilman Charles Ratcliff is here this evening? (*ad-lib with them as LARS approaches. At this point LOU ENTERS front and lingers near front*)

LARS: Who are you looking for?

MCMANSHON: Councilman Ratcliff.

LARS: Yea he's sitting right over....

* *At this point the audience at table may have informed McManshon that Ratcliff left, went to bathroom etc... McManshon can inform Lars that he knows etc...*

LARS: Who are you?

MCMANSHON: I'm Special Investigator McManshon.

LOU begins walking toward them.

LARS: Special investigator? What's that?

MCMANSHON: I'm not in a position to say at this point.

LARS: What position or point can you say?

MCMANSHON: I can say I'm here on special business with the Councilman and that's pretty much all I can say. If you'll excuse me. (*crosses away -toward back*)

LOU: Who's that?

LARS: An investigator on special business.

LOU: What kind of special business?

LARS: He couldn't say.

LOU: You don't say.

LARS: He didn't, that's for sure. Did say he's looking for Ratcliff.

LOU: Ratcliff? Uh-oh!

ETHYL and ELLA enter

ETHYL: ..so I told the doctor that I'm on a fixed income and I just can't afford to be gallivanting all over town for my medicine. And you know, he has this foreign accent that's so thick, I just can't understand him!

ELLA: Where is your doctor from?

ETHYL: Kentucky

McManshon approaches the ladies.

MCMANSHON: Excuse me. Have you seen Councilman Ratcliff?

ETHYL: No, I don't get cable. It's too expensive. I'm on a fixed income you see.

ELLA: No Ethyl, he means the Councilman that was here. The one all dressed up with the big scarf.

ETHYL: Oh! Wayne Newton?

ELLA: No Ethyl, he's supposed to be Elvis.

ETHYL: Elvis? I thought Elvis was dead. *(they continue on to seats)*

TANYA: *(overhearing crosses to McManshon)* Excuse me, but I'm Councilman's personal assistant Tanya. Can I help you?

MCMANSHON: I'm Special Investigator McManshon with the local Federal Bureau. I have special business to discuss with Mr. Ratcliff.

Lou and Lars are away from McManshon & Tanya but close enough to eavesdrop.

LOU: *(to Lars)* Federal Bureau?

LARS: What is he? A cop?

LOU: Worse than that. I seen something about these guys on the O'Riley Factor. They're top secret Feds. Big time covert types.

LARS: Like the Black Helicopter guys?

LOU: Worse than that.

LARS: Really. Who could be worse than that?

LOU: Insurance salesmen.

TANYA: *(talking to McManshon)* I see. Well, the Councilman is indisposed at this moment. Is there something I

ACT I 25

can help you with?

MCMANSHON: It's a special personal matter concerning the Councilman... personally.

LARS: Sounds personal.

TANYA: If you don't mind my asking, doesn't the Federal Bureau concern Federal matters? So this 'personal matter' would be something more of a Federal matter?

MCMANSHON: I'm not at liberty to say.

TANYA: Are you at liberty to tell me if the Councilman is being investigated?

LOU: Of course he is! (*crosses to them*) I know a guy who has a nephew who said that Ratcliff is as shady as the day is long! He has his hand in all sorts of crooked obligations!

TANYA: I beg your pardon!

LOU: I'm telling ya, this element remain deal is just the top of the ice cube! So, why don't you go on there young lady and fetch your boss! Let's all see justice in action when this here Fed plants the handcuffs on him! Go on!

TANYA: I'll go and find him. (*crosses and exits*)

MCMANSHON: If you please Mr... Mr...uh..

LOU: Braunhorst. Louis Braunhorst.

MCMANSHON: Mr. Braunhorst, (*takes out NOTEPAD from jacket noting Lou's name in it*) as I have stated, this is a private matter. I don't wish to call any more undue attention..

LOU: Hey pal! What are you doin' there? What are you writing in that book?

MCMANSHON: I'm just not very good at remembering names and I wanted to make note of it.

LOU: I'll have you know, I'm a God paying, tax fearing citizen! I didn't spend six months in the Coast Guard, protecting our shores, to have my name written down in some notebook!

MCMANSHON: I'm sorry Mr. Brownshorts..

LOU: Braunhorst! It's Braunhorst!

MCMANSHON: I told you I'm terrible at remembering names.

LOU: Sure, write down my name in that book and the next thing I know, my checking account will end up with subpoena! My mail will get censured and my dog gets neutered! I've seen it happen. I know a guy at work whose neighbor's friend got a chip planted in his brain while he was the barber! It happened after his name got put in one of these books. Believe me fella! I know!

MCMANSHON: I assure you, sir, that writing your name down here will only refresh my memory, not neuter your pet.

LOU: We'll see about that. Bad things happen when you people are around. Really bad things. You just wait and see!

TANYA enters very quickly looking a bit frazzled.

TANYA: Inspector McManshon! Charlie uh... Councilman Ratcliff is uh.... Could you come here for a second?

MCMANSHON: Sure. *(quickly crosses and goes out)*

LOU: Did anyone else here get their name put in his book? *(to audience)*

As the audience responds, Lou and Fannie Mae re-enter in front.

ERIC: Mr. Braunhorst, I don't think the Agent there has anything to do with the type of.. covert operations. More than likely, it has to do with funds.

LOU: Fun? What kind of fun does he expect to have at this place?

TRISH: No "funds" as in *money*. It was just a matter of time before the feds caught up with Ratcliff.

LOU: You mean this here Agent is a funds fed?

ERIC: Possibly. There's speculation this real estate deal is just a bunch of smoke and mirrors that will ultimately move the Ratcliff up into a new tax bracket.

LOU: Tax racket? I knew that guy was no good.

FANNIE MAE: Excuse me, Mr. Lawson, where on earth did you hear this nonsense? *(crossing toward them)*

ERIC: It's been all over the local blogging communities.

GEORGE: What did he say about the logging community?

McMANSHON enters followed by TANYA.

MCMANSHON: Excuse me! Everyone? I'm going to have to contain this area as a crime scene.

FANNIE MAE: Crime scene?

TANYA: Charlie is dead! *(buries her face in her hands weeping)*

MCMANSHON: Let's keep the details secret.

TANYA: He was strangled with his scarf! In the bathroom!

MCMANSHON: OK, See that's not keeping this secret.

LOU: Ratcliff is dead?

LARS: You mean the Elvis guy?

LOU: Died in the bathroom? *(laughs)*

LARS: How perfect! I mean, not perfect that the guy's dead. But that he was dressed as Elvis and died in the.. ah nevermind!

ETHYL: What are they saying?

LARS: We're saying that Elvis has left the building.

MCMANSHON: Since there is hypothetically, the chance of foul play at work, I must ask that you all remain in this area.

LOU: Wait a minute. I thought you were just a Funds Fed.

MCMANSHON: Sir, I am a Federal law enforcement official. First and foremost.

LARS: I guess you're in a position to say now, huh?

MCMANSHON: Yes. I am now in that position. I will also need to know the names of anyone who was near, around or about the restroom area. Specifically, around the time councilman, Ratcliff was in there. (*pulling out his Notebook*)

LOU: Be careful, he's got this notebook out! Watch out for him writing your name down in that thing.

FANNIE MAE: Before any name writing, I think we need a moment or two here to collect ourselves. After all, this news is tragic and Charles was a dear friend and neighbor to some of us.

MCMANSHON: I see. (*jots something down*) Very well.

FANNIE MAE: If we could just have a little time to let this.. sink in, before you begin... doing whatever it is you're going to be doing.

MCMANSHON: Certainly. I understand.

LOU: What a bunch of baloney this is! Who needs time to let it sink in! The guy deserved what he got!

McManshon writes something down in notebook. Lou catches this out of the corner of his eye.

LOU: Scratch that. I don't mean that liberally. You don't have to write what I said.. cause what I meant is... maybe we should take some time and uh... think about what we're saying before we uh.. yea.

MCMANSHON: All right. I will give you some time. I'll make use of the time by collecting any evidence. Again, I must ask that no one leaves. Also, I must ask that no one say anything to anyone outside of these confines.

LOU: And these would be the confines outside, outside right? Not here inside inside?

MCMANSHON: Inside and outside. All right Mrs. Holmes if you would like to proceed.

FANNIE MAE: I move for a (15) minute recess. All those in favor? All those opposed?

ACT 2

To start the ACT McManshon will pick up the microphone and speak.

MCMANSHON: If I could have everyone's attention? Thank you. As you may or may not know, I am Special Investigator McManshon. I am an official Agent with the Bureau and until local law authorities arrive, I am in charge.

ELLA: So, what happened?

MCMANSHON: That's currently under investigation.

ELLA: I realize that smarty pants, what exactly is it that you are investigating? I mean, was he murdered? Did he slip and fall and bump his head? What?

MCMANSHON: Well, without exposing too many details; Mr. Ratcliff was found in the Men's room, bereft of life.

GEORGE: Benefit his wife? I didn't think he was married.

LOU: Let's cut the tedious stuff and talk about the real issue! Somebody here is a killer!

ETHYL: Who's a killer?

ELLA: No one yet Ethyl. We're talking about the gentleman they found dead in the Men's room.

ETHYL: Oh! Well, that must have been the gentleman we heard yelling when we were in the powder room.

MCMANSHON: Excuse me? Did you say "yelling"?

ELLA: I thought it was some man singing.

ETHYL: It sounded like yelling to me.

MCMANSHON: Yelling? You heard yelling?

ELLA: No Ethyl, I think it was singing. It sounded like..

ETHYL: Like blue murder if you ask me.

MCMANSHON: You heard a man yelling...?

ELLA: More like Blue Hawaii. I don't know. It may have been yelling. But a very musical yelling.

MCMANSHON: Pardon me, ladies? You heard..

ETHYL: Although most of the music these days sounds like yelling. Especially that Screamo and Death Metal.. so he could have been singing..

MCMANSHON: Excuse me? (*snapping his fingers*) Ladies! Ladies? Can I get your attention for just a moment?

ELLA: Why sure. It's a free country.

MCMANSHON: Am I to understand you heard some

ACT 2

type yelling coming from the restroom?

ELLA: Sure. You can understand that, if you want.

MCMANSHON: So you were in the same proximity, the restrooms, and heard a man's voice, yelling or singing, and this sound was coming from the Men's Room?

ELLA: Yes. Ethyl and I were in the ladies' room and we heard sounds.

LOU: Was it yelling? Like somebody screaming "Help me! Somebody help me! I'm being murdered"? or was it more like, "Die you dog! Die!"

MCMANSHON: Mr. Brown-schwartz..

LOU: Braunhorst! Criminetly fella, you wrote it down.

MCMANSHON: Yes, Braunhorst, sir if you please..

FANNIE MAE: Lou why don't you let Agent McMan conduct the...

MCMANSHON: McManshon.

FANNIE MAE: Yes, McManshon, conduct the investigation?

LOU: That's fine Fannie Mae, but it don't take no Special Investment agent to construct it. These ladies may have some primo info.

MCMANSHON: Very true, but we must also open up other scenarios that may be relevant to other people. Other people who were out of the room at the same time as Mr. Ratcliff.

LARS: Well who was out of the room at that time?

LOU: I wouldn't know. I was out of the room.

MCMANSHON: And where were you?

LARS: He was outside the confines.

MCMANSHON: He was where?

LOU: I went outside to get some air. These meetings get my blood boiling. You see, I have hyper-tendons. The doctor told me when I get too worked up, I need to cool down and breathe a bit or else I'll keel over.

LARS: That's a fact. I saw him outside breathing. I went out to get his acorns.

MCMANSHON: His acorns?

LARS: Yea. When the covert black helicopters buzz his house they blow all the acorns off the oaks into the Michaels yard.

MCMANSHON: I see. That makes perfect sense.

LARS: I saw Fannie Mae outside too. She was also breathing.

MCMANSHON: Of course. Breathing is important, but if..

ERIC: Excuse me, Agent McManshon? I'm Eric Lawson, I don't mean to interrupt but actually, you see, I'm currently finishing Law School and studying for the bar, so

I am familiar with criminal procedures and Homicide investigations but I must say, I'm not familiar with a Federal Agents conducting Murder Investigations.

MCMANSHON: Ah, well, actually, I was here on a particular matter that involved Mr. Ratcliff. And now that we have a "new" matter involving Mr. Ratcliff, I mustn't overlook the possibility that these matters are related.

TRISH: Did you say *related*, Agent McManshon?

FANNIE MAE: That's *Mrs*. Lawson. The almost lawyer's wife. She's quite a..

TRISH: Some sources report that Councilman Ratcliff stood to gain a great deal of money, money from certain real estate developers and contractors, money passed under the table if he would pass the power to seize land. Land we currently live upon.

MCMANSHON: I'm not at liberty to..

TRISH: No one is at liberty when our liberties are taken from us.

LOU: You tell him sister!

TRISH: That's why you were here tonight, isn't it?! To charge Councilman Ratcliff with a laundry list of crimes!

TANYA: Charlie was the sweetest most innocent man in the world! He was trying to help you, people!

ELLA: Help? Help to displace an entire community?

Help tearing down our homes.

ETHYL: I'm too old to move. I'm on a fixed income!

FANNIE MAE: Well someone fixed Charlie didn't they? He won't be much help to anyone.

LOU: Nope, he'll need help learning to play a harp. Or swimming a lake of fire, whatever the case may be.

TRISH: The fact is Charlie Ratcliff had enough political clout to have our community declared an economic blight and stood to gain millions. And that's the real reason you were here! Isn't it?

MCMANSHON: I really can't say...

LOU: Well I can say that somebody here musta found out about all this business and kilt him!

LARS: Hey Lou, didn't you say you found out about it? Something about a guy who has a friend whose cousin or something?

LOU: Uh.. I really can't say at this point.

ELLA: Yes you did say, Lou! And you went outside just after Ratcliff went to the bathroom!

FANNIE MAE: So what Ella? You and Ethyl were in the restroom right next door? Who's to say one of you didn't slip over there and strangle him?

ELLA: Why would we do that?

LARS: Yea! Ethyl's on a fixed income.

ACT 2

TRISH: Excuse me Fannie Mae but I believe you also left this room for some time.

ERIC: If I may enter into evidence, quite a few people had opportunity and motive. But I'm sure special investigator McManshon is aware of this.

MCMANSHON: Thank you, Mr. Lawson, I am aware of all the facts. In fact, I would like to privately question some of the people..

TRISH: Privately question?

LOU: Yea! What with all this private business? If you're gunna question anybody it should be out here in the open. We know what happens when you government guys take people in a room to question them. You end up snowboarding everybody!

ERIC: Since this association meeting is still, for lack of

a better term, 'in session', why don't we open the questions to the community?

TRISH: Excellent idea! Since questions from the community are part of the associations' bylaws, we all should be invited to ask whatever we want.

MCMANSHON: I'm not sure that's a good idea. As I have pointed out...

LOU: Yea, yea, yea! Private top-secret matter, we know! But I'd feel a whole lot safer out here, among the people, and by the people, for the questioning. If you know what I mean.

MCMANSHON: If that's what you wish. Let's open this up to the floor.

FANNIE MAE: I see this as a big mistake. But.. all those in favor?

(*ALL OF BOARD*) AYE!

FANNIE MAE: All those opposed? Go ahead Agent, it's all yours.

MCMANSHON: Thank you. If we could keep this session secret for the time being and..

TRISH: OK does anyone have any questions?

(*NOTE: IT SOMETIMES TAKES A WHILE FOR THE AUDIENCE TO CATCH ON THEY CAN ASK THE CHARACTERS QUESTIONS. IT MAY TAKE A
LITTLE PROMPTING BUT ONCE THEY CATCH ON - IT SHOULD START ROLLING - IT MAY BE BEST TO HAVE THE DIRECTOR SIGNAL THE ACTORS TO WRAP IT UP - ONCE ENOUGH QUESTIONS HAVE BEEN ASKED
- MCMANSHON CAN WRAP IT UP BY SAYING "TWO MORE QUESTIONS, ONE MORE QUESTION" ETC.. AND THEN TO BRING THE PLAY BACK -
MCMANSHON WILL CONTINUE BELOW..*)

MCMANSHON: Just one more question...

LOU: I have a question! How are we supposed to make heads or tails of these questions? The fact is.. well, we don't know any clues or facts now do we? We know

Councilman Elvis got killed, strangled or whatever.. but did anybody look for any clues?

MCMANSHON: I did secure a few pieces of potential evidence.

LOU: Like what? And DON'T say that you're not at library to say! Enough of this secret stuff!!

MCMANSHON: All right. Well, what I can reveal is that there appeared to be an item missing from Mr. Ratcliff's scarf. Also, I found a foreign object on the floor not too far from the body.

LOU: Foreign object?! What country you reckon it was from?

ERIC: Agent McManshon? Can you be any more specific about these items.

MCMANSHON: Not at this time.

ELLA: Oh for heavens sakes! I've had it up to here with this business! What kind of outfit do you work for mister? What kind of organization keeps information from the people?

LOU: He probably works with the liberal media! MSNBC or somebody! Or maybe he's in some secret society! Like the Knights Templar of the round table or the Masonites, Shriners or Amway! Those kind who topple Governments and assimilate foreign debutantes!

MCMANSHON: It's my job to keep things quiet so that

the general population doesn't get overworked and blow everything out of proportion!

LOU: Who's blowing things out of proportion?! There's a killer here and if you don't start doing your job, then there's no tellin' who'll be killed next! It could be her or him or me or you! It may start here in this place and next thing you know, the whole street is murdered. And then he moves on to the next block and the next!

MCMANSHON: All right fine! If it will help, I can tell you this   Yes, I was following a trail of a questionable real estate deal. A dirty money trail that was paved from real estate development. We had obtained a secret video of Councilman Ratcliff meeting with some real estate players where certain illegal matters were discussed.

ERIC: We were right! Yes!

MCMANSHON: Yes you were. But, this video came from an unrelated investigation into a different matter. A private detective brought it to our attention when he heard the "discussion" on tape.

TRISH: Private Detective? What was he investigating?

MCMANSHON: Sorry, but that's where my information must end.

ERIC: Would this information concerns someone other than Councilman Ratcliff? Someone else here in this room?

MCMANSHON: I can't say and that's all I can say.

TRISH: It shouldn't be too hard to figure out.

LOU: I think you're onto something. I betcha Ratcliff was double-crossing somebody with this deal and they got a little peeved. And this peeved party made his Elvis dream true to life by killin him in the can.

ERIC: Private investigators usually take cases of infidelity or insurance fraud.

TRISH: So while looking into one of those, stumbled upon this Ratcliff-gate. So which one? Infidelity or insurance fraud?

LOU: I say we vote.

FANNIE MAE: We what?

LOU: Vote! Like in all these dag-blasted meetings, where you all are voting on junk. *Aye* for this and *nay* on that! But now we vote for what we think happened and who made it happen.

ERIC: Lou may have something here. You know in the judicial system they have grand juries, simply a group of people who decide if a case has enough merit to go to trial. I may be stretching that premise just a bit, but in principle, it's the same.

ETHYL: What are we doing?

LARS: I think we're voting on something.

FANNIE MAE: You want to put it a vote?

ERIC: I think it should be conducted like a traditional jury
vote. Where everyone writes down their vote and we collect them.

FANNIE MAE: Writes down their vote?

LARS: What are we voting for?

ERIC: It's fairly obvious that Agent McManshon has a propensity to keep the details of this event 'secret'. A man was killed here tonight and there is overwhelming motive as well as numerous opportunities, and since the good agent won't share his information, perhaps there are others here who have enough information to form a logical conclusion.

LARS: Right. But what are we voting for?

LOU: Did someone weed whack your brain boy? Vote for who you think killed Ratcliff!

TRISH: Right! Now everyone has a piece of paper at their association tables. Just for fun, let's review the facts and write down the top suspect!

ERIC: And the facts are that most of us were here when Councilman Ratcliff left. Some were out of the room. Who among those individuals had the appropriate motive to strangle the Councilman?

TRISH: (*any additional voting instructions*)

ACT 2

At the conclusion of voting.

FANNIE MAE: Well that went smoothly.

TRISH: Yes it did actually and I think we got a lot of interesting conclusions. In fact, there were quite a few people here tonight who shed light on some fascinating information.

MCMANSHON: Actually, I would like to keep some of the details..

ELLA: If you say "secret" I'll personally kick you in the kneecap!

LOU: Amen Ella! I'm fed up to here with all this secret schmeekret business! That's how this whole thing started! Secret real estate deals and secret out of order letters and outside confines!

ELLA: There's something bigger going on here than meets the eye!

ERIC: I have to concur. Something big that apparently can be explained by two small items. An item missing from Councilman Ratcliff scarf and a foreign object found on the floor.

TRISH: I think if we knew what those objects were it would help. Wouldn't they Agent McManshon?

MCMANSHON: I'm not a liberty to say.

ELLA -LOU -ERIC TRISH: Aw! Come on! For crying out loud! etc...

FANNIE MAE: George!

GEORGE: What? (*stands up*) Should I continue?

FANNIE MAE: What's that on your jacket? (*she stands and plucks a small item from jacket*) A sequin?

GEORGE: What? You're seeking? You're seeking what?

FANNIE MAE: Do you have your hearing aid turned off again?

GEORGE: Huh? No. The battery went dead. I thought I had a new one but I lost it somewhere.

FANNIE MAE: Maybe on the floor of the men's room?

GEORGE: The door of the men's room?

LOU George! It was George!

ELLA: It's the sequin from Ratcliff's scarf!

GEORGE: What?

TRISH: I get it now! The private detective! Ratcliff was having an affair! That's where the incriminating video came from!

LOU: Having an affair with who?

TRISH: With Fannie Mae!

TANYA: He was not! He told me he dumped her months ago!

FANNIE MAE: Is that what he told you?

ACT 2

TANYA: Yes! That's what he told me!

ERIC: So Mr. Holmes did you hire a private detective to follow your wife?

LOU: Sure he did! He found out about the trisket between Fannie Mae and Ratcliff and then strung him up in the john!

ELLA: The battery from his hearing aid came out on the floor and the sequin popped off the scarf and stuck to his jacket!

FANNIE MAE: George! You have some explaining to do!

GEORGE: Actually, no. It's *my wife* who has some explaining to do. Isn't that correct Agent McManshon?

MCMANSHON: You don't want to keep this secret anymore George?

GEORGE: No. There have been enough secrets for now.

LOU: Hey! How come you can hear?

GEORGE: I'm not a liberty to say.

MCMANSHON: What I am now at liberty to say is that Mrs. Holmes was having a liaison with Councilman Ratcliff. Mr. Holmes hired a private detective who obtained evidence not only of the affair but of an illicit real estate business deal. Mr. Holmes brought the matter to our attention. As we began building our case. It seems that all parties concerned began to get greedy which quickly ended the secret romance.

ELLA: So he did dump her!

TANYA: I told you!

MCMANSHON: However the real estate deal was still in the works. But with Mrs. Holmes only getting a fraction of the original bargain, she threatened to expose the whole deal and that brought Councilman Ratcliff here this evening to negotiate a new deal.

ELLA: But she killed him instead!

LOU: And tried to pin it on George!

ELLA: The jealous husband!

LARS: So she took a sequin off the Elvis scarf and stuck it on George and then took his new hearing aid battery and dropped it on the floor!

ELLA: What do you have to say for yourself Fannie Mae!

FANNIE MAE: I'd rather not say at this point. I'd like to speak to an attorney.

McManshon turns Fannie Mae around and places handcuffs on her.

MCMANSHON: Let's go. (*begins leading her out*)

FANNIE MAE: So Mr. Lawson? How soon till you take the bar exam?

ERIC: In a month actually.

TRISH: What are you doing?!

ERIC: This would be a great first case! (*He follows them out with Trish -ad-libbing back and forth as they exit*)

LOU: Justice is served!

LARS: Actually not yet Lou, I need to get your acorns for
you.

Lou and Lars Exit ad-libbing. ELLA and ETHYL cross to GEORGE.

ELLA: So you mean to tell me, you could hear this whole time?

GEORGE: Hear the bells chime?

Ella, Ethyl and George exit ad-libbing. Tanya follows behind them. - the end

AFTERWORD

PRODUCTION NOTES In the original production, **A Plot Of Murder** was performed in Banquet room. However, the setting is a basic "board meeting" and can be adapted to presented on a Stage - as sometimes Board Meeting are. To keep the interactive part of the play - other than the Board Members who would be seated on the Stage, the other characters should be seated in the audience -to convey the feeling that "everyone" is involved in the meeting. Setting was simply a Meeting style - long table with chairs. A pitcher of water with cups. And if possible a live microphone. A prop microphone can be used if needed.

BOOKS BY THIS AUTHOR

Last Call At Chez Mort

A Night Club in the 1940s is the scene of a bizarre death. Was it an accident or was it murder? Inspector Constantine could pin it on any one of these mugs. The gangster, the showgirl, the French guy, the Russian with a hatchet. Will he pick the right one?

An Audition For A Murder

A Theatre group is holding auditions for a Murder Mystery called "Death of A Disco Dancer". One of the actors mysteriously dies. Luckily the playwright has invited a detective to the auditions. Can the case be solved? Can the show be cast?

A Murder Has Been Renounced

A couple's car breaks down on a dark and stormy night. A nearby estate offers shelter and an oddball group of guests all behaving very strangely. The phone lines are down and a necklace is stolen, shots are fired, a guest is strangled. You know, the usual fare.

To Wake The Dead

Renown Mystery writer Fred Finnegan has died under unusual circumstances and all his friends have gathered at his wake. Was Fred murdered by someone at the wake? Because Fred's ghost shows up and he's dying to find out who dun it!

Made in the USA
Las Vegas, NV
24 July 2021